Introdu

Expressing gratitude doesn't require money. It doesn't require much thought or effort, but it can change our whole outlook on life.

Last year, I started keeping a gratitude journal—a small journal where I recorded a few blessings from each day. I was experiencing some health problems at the time and this simple exercise helped me to keep a positive, thankful attitude while struggling with pain and discomfort. Once those health problems were resolved, I had seen such benefit in recording my blessings every day that I continued doing it.

I'm all about keeping things simple, so I've been using a one-line-a-day journal like this one. Every morning, when I first wake up, I read my Bible, pray, and write down at least one line of blessings from the past day. Some days it's easier to come up with blessings than others, but I can always come up with at least a few good things from the day before—even if it was a hard day.

Starting my day by recounting the blessings from the previous day puts me in a different state of mind. Instead of focusing on the discouraging or difficult things in life (and we all have some of those, don't we?), writing down my blessings helps me to reflect on all that's good and beautiful in my life.

No matter what season of life you're in or what burdens you're carrying, there is always, always, always something to be thankful for. When you start looking for things to be thankful for, you often begin to notice many wonderful things that you hadn't before. And truly, living with an attitude of gratitude will not only transform your outlook—it just might change your entire life!

Choose gratitude today!

Crystal Paine

JANUARY

Start the Year with Purpose

Without goals, you have nothing that you're aiming for. Goals give you passion, purpose, motivation, and drive.

A WEEK OF GRATITUDE

8...

....

9...

....

10...

....

11...

....

12...

....

13...

....

14...

....

Write your
goals down
and put them
in a very
conspicuous
place.

Consider your priorities and
where you want to be in a
year from now. Think about
the time you'll have to invest.
Then, choose 3-5 specific
goals for the year.

8

A WEEK OF GRATITUDE

15. . . . .

. . . .

16. . . . .

. . . .

17. . . . .

. . . .

18. . . . .

. . . .

19. . . . .

. . . .

20. . . . .

. . . .

21. . . . .

. . . .

Once you have yearly goals in place, take some time to map out a plan for how you're going to accomplish your goals. Write down the specific steps you will take each month to get where you hope to be in a year from now.

A WEEK OF GRATITUDE

22...

....

23...

....

24...

....

25...

....

26...

....

27...

....

28...

....

Whatever happens,
do not give up.
If you get knocked
down, pick yourself
back up, dust
yourself off,
and keep going.

A WEEK OF GRATITUDE

29 ....

....

30 ....

....

31 ....

....

....

....

....

....

....

....

"The secret of getting ahead is getting started. The secret of getting started is breaking your complex overwhelming tasks into small manageable tasks, and then starting on the first one."

—MARK TWAIN

Little bit by little bit, you will change your life... all because you set goals, broke them down into bite-sized pieces, and followed through with them.

FEBRUARY

Appreciate Relationships

At the end of your life, the money you made won't matter. The house you lived in won't matter. The car you drove won't matter. The clothes you wore won't matter. What will matter is the lives you impacted and the people you invested in.

16

A WEEK OF GRATITUDE

1. ....

....

2. ....

....

3. ....

....

4. ....

....

5. ....

....

6. ....

....

7. ....

....

When you look back on each day, if you made memories as a family, invested in things that matter, and haven't completely exhausted yourself, be encouraged and happy.

Don't become obsessed with following your routine or plans to a tee at the expense of your relationships with those you love.

A WEEK OF GRATITUDE

8.

9.

10.

11.

12.

13.

14.

"How you make
others feel about
themselves says a
lot about you."
—UNKNOWN

A WEEK OF GRATITUDE

15. . . . .

. . . .

16. . . . .

. . . .

17. . . . .

. . . .

18. . . . .

. . . .

19. . . . .

. . . .

20. . . . .

. . . .

21. . . . .

. . . .

Being willing to ask forgiveness and admit when you are wrong is hard, but it's one of the best things you can do for any relationship.

A WEEK OF GRATITUDE

22 ....

....

23 ....

....

24 ....

....

25 ....

....

26 ....

....

27 ....

....

28 ....

....

A community is
where people feel
welcomed, heard,
accepted, and a
part of something.
You are unique.
You have a story.
You have a
purpose.

MARCH

Simplify Your Life

If you have a full schedule, you won't naturally find a lot of margin or breathing room in your life. Instead, you have to be intentional about cultivating it.

A WEEK OF GRATITUDE

1. ....

....

2. ....

....

3. ....

....

4. ....

....

5. ....

....

6. ....

....

7. ....

....

Practice the one in, one out rule. Whenever you get something new, make a habit of also getting rid of something you no longer need or use. This will help keep some of the clutter at bay and will remind you how blessed you are!

A WEEK OF GRATITUDE

8 ....

....

9 ....

....

10 ....

....

11 ....

....

12 ....

....

13 ....

....

14 ....

....

"Gratitude turns what
we have into enough."
—MELODY BEATTIE

A WEEK OF GRATITUDE

15...

....

16...

....

17...

....

18...

....

19...

....

20...

....

21...

....

Instead of packing every hour of the day with an activity or project, schedule in at least two hours of margin time. This is buffer time to allow for the interruptions that are bound to happen.

If you don't have two hours' worth of interruptions in a day, you can use the extra time to do something relaxing or refreshing.

A WEEK OF GRATITUDE

22 ....

....

23 ....

....

24 ....

....

25 ....

....

26 ....

....

27 ....

....

28 ....

....

If you de-clutter one area a day for only ten minutes, you'll be amazed at how much you can accomplish in a few weeks.

A WEEK OF GRATITUDE

29 ....

....

30 ....

....

31 ....

....

Have nothing in your
house that you do not
know to be useful, or
believe to be beautiful.
—WILLIAM MORRIS

APRIL

Create Space to Breathe

Ask yourself what truly refreshes you. Make a list of the things that come to mind, and then think through how you can incorporate some of these things into your everyday life.

A WEEK OF GRATITUDE

1 ....

....

2 ....

....

3 ....

....

4 ....

....

5 ....

....

6 ....

....

7 ....

....

I savor the morning quiet. It's when I think, read, pray, plan, write, breathe, and dream. When I begin the day with quiet, the whole day feels calmer.

8. ....

....

9. ....

....

10. ....

....

11. ....

....

12. ....

....

13. ....

....

14. ....

....

Breathe. Soak up the quiet. Savor the stillness. Even if it's just for two minutes.

A WEEK OF GRATITUDE

15..

....

16..

....

17..

....

18..

....

19..

....

20..

....

21..

....

"If you're always racing to the next moment, what happens to the one you're in?"

—UNKNOWN

A WEEK OF GRATITUDE

22 ....

....

23 ....

....

24 ....

....

25 ....

....

26 ....

....

27 ....

....

28 ....

....

If we don't allow white space to breathe and refresh, but instead pack every moment of every day full to the brim with to-do's and projects, our lives will feel chaotic, disorderly, and exhausting.

A WEEK OF GRATITUDE

29 ....

....

30 ....

....

....

....

....

....

....

....

....

M A Y

Dream, Plan, and Prepare for the Future

What are your goals in life? Are you thinking long-term or just trying to live through the next hour? If your goal is just to survive, that's probably not going to give you a lot of excitement about life nor fuel much passion for existence.

8 ....

....

9 ....

....

10 ....

....

11 ....

....

12 ....

....

13 ....

....

14 ....

....

You'll never make any progress if you stop dreaming. You'll never get anywhere if you feel like taking a step in the right direction is a pointless exercise.

A WEEK OF GRATITUDE

15..

....

16..

....

17..

....

18..

....

19..

....

20..

....

21..

....

"What you do today
is important because
you are exchanging a
day of your life for it."

—UNKNOWN

A WEEK OF GRATITUDE

22 ....

....

23 ....

....

24 ....

....

25 ....

....

26 ....

....

27 ....

....

28 ....

....

There are many
good things in life
that you can invest
your life in, but you
can't come close to
trying to do them all.

A WEEK OF GRATITUDE

29 ....

....

30 ....

....

31 ....

....

....

....

....

....

....

....

....

Figure out what the best things are for YOU and wrap your life, time, and energy around those things.

JUNE

Take Time to Smell the Roses

There is so much wonder and beauty in each day. The smile of a little child, the colors of a flower, the smell of soup cooking... if we take time to notice and pay attention, there are beautiful things all around us.

A WEEK OF GRATITUDE

1. . . . .

. . . .

2. . . . .

. . . .

3. . . . .

. . . .

4. . . . .

. . . .

5. . . . .

. . . .

6. . . . .

. . . .

7. . . . .

. . . .

"The happiest people don't have the best of everything; they just make the best of everything."

—UNKNOWN

8 ....

....

9 ....

....

10 ....

....

11 ....

....

12 ....

....

13 ....

....

14 ....

....

Even in the darkest, most disappointing days, there is always a glimmer of light. No matter how difficult the situation you are in, as long as you're breathing, there is hope.

A WEEK OF GRATITUDE

15. ....

....

16. ....

....

17. ....

....

18. ....

....

19. ....

....

20. ....

....

21. ....

....

Take time to breathe.
You need to soak
up the sunshine,
the beauty, the
smells, the sounds,
the wonder of life
teeming around you
in all directions.

A WEEK OF GRATITUDE

22 . . . .

. . . .

23 . . . .

. . . .

24 . . . .

. . . .

25 . . . .

. . . .

26 . . . .

. . . .

27 . . . .

. . . .

28 . . . .

. . . .

Stopping to smell the roses
is not only rejuvenating, it's
imperative if you want to lead
a healthy, well-balanced life.

A WEEK OF GRATITUDE

29 ....

....

30 ....

....

....

....

....

....

....

....

....

Don't let disappointment swallow up your hope, your joy,
or your life. Look for the beauty in every day.

There is *always* something to be grateful for. No matter your circumstances, no matter your situation, if you start looking for things to appreciate, you'll begin to find them all around you.

JULY

Cultivate Beauty

Cultivate beauty, art, and creativity in your home and life. A few of my favorite ways to do this are listening to music with rich depth, trying yummy new recipes, watching movies and reading books with great story lines, and burning delicious-smelling candles. Such simple things inspire and enrich my life.

A WEEK OF GRATITUDE

1. ....

   ....

2. ....

   ....

3. ....

   ....

4. ....

   ....

5. ....

   ....

6. ....

   ....

7. ....

   ....

"Being happy doesn't mean everything is perfect. It means you've decided to see beyond the imperfections."

—UNKNOWN

A WEEK OF GRATITUDE

8 ....

....

9 ....

....

10 ....

....

11 ....

....

12 ....

....

13 ....

....

14 ....

....

One of the reasons I aim to always have some kind of handwork project going—be it knitting, embroidery, or something else—is because it gives me a sense of fulfillment to create with my hands. And this creativity often breeds creativity and energy in other areas of my life.

A WEEK OF GRATITUDE

15 ....

....

16 ....

....

17 ....

....

18 ....

....

19 ....

....

20 ....

....

21 ....

....

We can't always change our circumstances, but we can always change our attitude.

A WEEK OF GRATITUDE

22 ....

....

23 ....

....

24 ....

....

25 ....

....

26 ....

....

27 ....

....

28 ....

....

Choose to make the most of wherever you find yourself. Embrace the moments. Live with zest. Find joy in the little things.

A WEEK OF GRATITUDE

29 ....

....

30 ....

....

31 ....

....

AUGUST

Invest in Friendships

When you live
your life with
outstretched
arms, you are
richly blessed
in return.

A WEEK OF GRATITUDE

1 ....

....

2 ....

....

3 ....

....

4 ....

....

5 ....

....

6 ....

....

7 ....

....

You shouldn't give so that you'll get blessings (because otherwise it's not true giving at all!), but I guarantee that you will lead a much more fulfilled and joyful life if you spend your life pouring it out for others.

A WEEK OF GRATITUDE

8 ....

....

9 ....

....

10 ....

....

11 ....

....

12 ....

....

13 ....

....

14 ....

....

"Two are better than one, because they have a good reward for their toil. For if they fall, one will lift up his fellow. But woe to him who is alone when he falls and has not another to lift him up!"

—Ecclesiastes 4:9-10 ESV

A WEEK OF GRATITUDE

15...

....

16...

....

17...

....

18...

....

19...

....

20...

....

21...

....

When you take the
focus off of yourself and
begin reaching out to
other people, you'll start
to forget about your
problems and worries.
And you'll probably find
you have a lot more joy
and fulfillment, too!

A WEEK OF GRATITUDE

22 . . . .

. . . .

23 . . . .

. . . .

24 . . . .

. . . .

25 . . . .

. . . .

26 . . . .

. . . .

27 . . . .

. . . .

28 . . . .

. . . .

In this increasingly virtual world of social media, being intentional to foster real-life relationships with depth, meaning, and authenticity is so important.

A WEEK OF GRATITUDE

29 ....

....

30 ....

....

31 ....

....

....

....

....

....

....

....

....

True balance is not spending exactly equal amounts of time on every facet of your life, but it's making sure that, over the course of a few months, you are giving focused attention to each important area in your life, and that the unimportant things aren't creeping in and crowding out what really matters.

SEPTEMBER

Improve Your Mind

Constantly seek to be
improving your mind through
reading, thinking through
issues, and learning new
things. Don't let your brain
turn to "mush."

A WEEK OF GRATITUDE

1 ....

....

2 ....

....

3 ....

....

4 ....

....

5 ....

....

6 ....

....

7 ....

....

Instead of
spending time
fretting over what
probably never
will be, redirect
that energy
into something
positive.

A WEEK OF GRATITUDE

8 ....

....

9 ....

....

10 ....

....

11 ....

....

12 ....

....

13 ....

....

14 ....

....

When you catch yourself worrying, try to instead pour that energy and time into something more productive: reading, writing, exercising, listening to an audiobook, cleaning, singing, or serving someone else.

A WEEK OF GRATITUDE

15. . . . .

. . . .

16. . . . .

. . . .

17. . . . .

. . . .

18. . . . .

. . . .

19. . . . .

. . . .

20. . . . .

. . . .

21. . . . .

. . . .

Take a class, learn a new skill, try a new recipe, experiment with a new do-it-yourself project, develop a new friendship, read a new kind of book, try a new fitness routine... the possibilities are endless.

A WEEK OF GRATITUDE

22 ....

....

23 ....

....

24 ....

....

25 ....

....

26 ....

....

27 ....

....

28 ....

....

"You are what you are,
and you are where
you are because of
what has gone into
your mind."
—ZIG ZIGLAR

A WEEK OF GRATITUDE

29 ....

....

30 ....

....

....

....

....

....

....

....

....

....

Challenge yourself to always be learning. This will not only inspire your creativity and motivate you to think outside the box, but it will also give you renewed zest and passion for life.

OCTOBER

Improve Your Health

Your health is one of your most important assets. Regular exercise and a proper diet reduce the risk of many diseases and improve your overall energy.

A WEEK OF GRATITUDE

1. ....

   ....

2. ....

   ....

3. ....

   ....

4. ....

   ....

5. ....

   ....

6. ....

   ....

7. ....

   ....

Instead of trying to overhaul your health overnight, work on instilling one new healthy habit each month. By taking it slowly, there's much more chance of the new habit turning into a lifelong change.

A WEEK OF GRATITUDE

8 ....

....

9 ....

....

10 ....

....

11 ....

....

12 ....

....

13 ....

....

14 ....

....

If you don't take the time to rest, you'll constantly be running on fumes.

Rearrange your schedule, turn off your electronics, do relaxing things before bed, go to bed early (if at all possible), take a 30-minute nap in the afternoon, or do whatever else it takes to make sure you are getting good sleep at least 5-6 nights each week.

A WEEK OF GRATITUDE

15. . . . .

. . . .

16. . . . .

. . . .

17. . . . .

. . . .

18. . . . .

. . . .

19. . . . .

. . . .

20. . . . .

. . . .

21. . . . .

. . . .

It's well been said, "Laughter is the best medicine." It's amazing how smiling, laughing, and seeing the humorous side of life can just make life more enjoyable—and give you much more zest for life!

A joyful heart is good medicine.
—Proverbs 17:22 ESV

A WEEK OF GRATITUDE

22 . . . .

. . . .

23 . . . .

. . . .

24 . . . .

. . . .

25 . . . .

. . . .

26 . . . .

. . . .

27 . . . .

. . . .

28 . . . .

. . . .

Exercise will refresh you; it will help you shed excess pounds that can be zapping your energy, and it will probably help you be more alert and focused. Plus, as a side benefit, it may help you sleep better at night!

A WEEK OF GRATITUDE

29 ....

....

30 ....

....

31 ....

....

....

....

....

....

....

....

Make exercise a priority; your current and future health
is worth the sacrifice of time and effort.

No matter where
you end up in life,
a hard-working,
persevering
attitude will be a
huge benefit.

"Comparison is the thief of joy."
—THEODORE ROOSEVELT

NOVEMBER

Count Your Blessings

There is always, always, always something to be thankful for. When you have a thankful, grateful spirit, you'll automatically have more joy, zest for life, and energy. It's the natural outflow of gratitude.

A WEEK OF GRATITUDE

1 ....

 ....

2 ....

 ....

3 ....

 ....

4 ....

 ....

5 ....

 ....

6 ....

 ....

7 ....

 ....

Choose gratitude today—even when it feels impossible. It might not change any of your circumstances, but I promise that it will transform your attitude and lift your spirits.

A WEEK OF GRATITUDE

8 ....

....

9 ....

....

10 ....

....

11 ....

....

12 ....

....

13 ....

....

14 ....

....

In everything give thanks.
—1 Thessalonians 5:16-18 NKJV

A WEEK OF GRATITUDE

15 ....

   ....

16 ....

   ....

17 ....

   ....

18 ....

   ....

19 ....

   ....

20 ....

   ....

21 ....

   ....

If you have a sturdy
roof over your
head, a closet with
some clothes in
it, a little food in
your fridge, and
family and friends
to hug, you are very
blessed today.

A WEEK OF GRATITUDE

22 ....

....

23 ....

....

24 ....

....

25 ....

....

26 ....

....

27 ....

....

28 ....

....

If I'm too busy to count my blessings, I'm just plain too busy. Life is full of blessings—even on the really difficult days.

29 ....

....

30 ....

....

....

....

....

....

....

....

....

It's a good thing to stop and express our gratitude—
we all have much to be thankful for.

DECEMBER

Be a Giver

A life of giving is born out of practicing the attitude of serving again and again until it becomes your natural response.

A WEEK OF GRATITUDE

1 ....

....

2 ....

....

3 ....

....

4 ....

....

5 ....

....

6 ....

....

7 ....

....

Our goal in living on a budget is not so we can continuously upgrade our lifestyle and always be buying bigger and better things. We want to manage our money wisely so we are able to give generously to others.

Live simply so others can simply live.

A WEEK OF GRATITUDE

8. ....
   ....

9. ....
   ....

10. ....
    ....

11. ....
    ....

12. ....
    ....

13. ....
    ....

14. ....
    ....

There's a world of need around us. If we are intentional in how we spend our money, we can be in a better position to help meet those needs. The more we save, the more we have to give.

A WEEK OF GRATITUDE

15..

....

16..

....

17..

....

18..

....

19..

....

20..

....

21..

....

Your efforts and my efforts might seem like a drop in the bucket when compared with all of the need that's out there. But collectively, we can make a huge impact.

A WEEK OF GRATITUDE

22 ....

....

23 ....

....

24 ....

....

25 ....

....

26 ....

....

27 ....

....

28 ....

....

The more you live for others, the more you step outside your comfort zone; the more you give freely and generously of your resources and time, the more you'll wake up feeling blessed, motivated, and inspired to live to the fullest!

140

A WEEK OF GRATITUDE

29 ....

....

30 ....

....

31 ....

....

....

....

....

....

....

....

"If you can't feed a hundred people, then just feed one."
—MOTHER TERESA

Live your life with outstretched arms.

A wife and homeschool mom of three, Crystal Paine is a bestselling author, business consultant, speaker, and the founder of MoneySavingMom.com. Started in 2007, Money Saving Mom® has since grown to be one of the top personal finance blogs on the web averaging over 1.5 million unique visitors per month.

Author of the New York Times bestselling book *Say Goodbye To Survival Mode: 9 Simple Strategies to Stress Less, Sleep More, and Restore Your Passion for Life*, Crystal's mission is to help women from all walks of life discover the freedom that comes from living with intention, simplicity, and generosity.

In addition to running her own business, she serves as a consultant to executives and business owners in the areas of brand development, online growth and social media strategy.

Crystal has contributed to articles in *Woman's Day* and *All You* magazines, appeared on Good Morning America and the 700 Club, and has been mentioned on The Today Show, National Public Radio, CNN, *USA Weekend*, *Shop Smart* magazine, *Real Simple* magazine, and numerous other local and national newspapers, radio, and television stations. She is also the author of the bestselling book, *The Money Saving Mom®'s Budget.*

Her motto is this: live simply, save aggressively, give generously. Through her books and blog she seeks to encourage women and families to wisely steward their time, energy, and finances so that, ultimately, they might be able to bless and give more to those in their community and around the world.